The More I Pray,

The More I Understand

God's Word

By: Carmel Adams

Christians everywhere are suffering because of
unanswered prayers. They do not understand how to
pray and receive answers from God.

The time to pray is now!
The time to understand is now!
The time to receive answers is now!

"Trust in the Lord with all of
thine heart and lean not unto thine own
understanding". (Proverbs 3:5)

My Personal experience is what I am
about to share with you.

The More I Pray

Pray the Word!

My love for praying has always been my number one priority. Praying about everything has birthed me a whole new experience from daily reading and studying God's word. Jesus said, "And he spake a parable unto them (disciples), to this end that men ought always to pray and not faint". (Luke 18:1) If we continue to pray in ignorance, we will not get our prayers answer. Especially, the difficult ones. The time has come for Christians everywhere to pray with understanding and teach other believers that they can get their prayers answered according to God's time, way, will, and purpose.

"Pray without ceasing."
1 Thessalonians 5:17

Pray that you will receive answers from God for whatever you need. In the Bible it quotes

"Confess your faults one to another, and pray one for another, that ye may be healed. The effectual fervent prayer of a righteous man availeth much power."

James 5:16

1. Elijah prayed, and the rain did not fall, then he prayed and the rain fell.
2. Moses prayed, God opened the red sea and rolled back the water for the Israelites to cross over.
3. Daniel prayed three times a day and was not eaten by the lion when he was thrown into the lion's den.
4. Prayed, worshiped, and danced before God and he became a man after God's own heart.,

The More I Pray

5. Samson prayed after he had his eyes plucked out by the Philistines, he later regained his strength and killed more people in his death than his life.
6. Jesus prayed in the Garden of Gethsemane just before he went to the cross and received divine strength to bear the agonizing pain of his crucifixion for our sins.
7. Jesus taught his disciples how to pray to receive the Holy Spirit and power. (Acts 1:8 2:4)
8. God Himself in the beginning prayed "let there be light and there was light" (Genesis 1:3)

The More I Pray

Table of Contents

The More I Pray

Preface

I have written this book out of the revelation that God has imparted to me while spending quality time with Him every day during my study periods. These truths will revolutionize your Spirit, soul, mind, and body. It will mold your heart, transform your mind and confirm your will to God's will. You will change the way you pray, think, talk, and act. You will receive more answers to your prayers and solutions for your problems. You will be able to face the giant circumstances in your life that seem to overwhelm you in TOTAL victory. As you continue to read, revelations will be divinely deposited into your Spiritual account supernaturally. Then your prayers will produce the power to change your whole natural ability into the supernatural being which God has intended for you to become. You will discover God's divine will for your life as you continue to spend time with Him in prayer and praying his word for his promises to come to pass in your life.

Introduction

At eleven years old I began reading my Bible with no one telling me to. I simply adored the stories in the scriptures. I would always memorize a few of them. Learning memory verses were what kept close to my heart. I would read, then study a verse, close my Bible, then try to say the whole verse without looking into the Bible. This learning method has helped me gain more understanding of many Bible verses. One of my favorite scriptures, "But seek ye first the kingdom of God, and his righteousness: and all these things shall be added unto you." (Matthew 6:33). I made this scripture the foundation for my life. When I was by myself, I would pray to God, when I could not find something I would say, "God can you please help me find it?" It was never a time He did answer. Since then I came to understand that He sees, knows, hears, cares, and answers prayers when you ask Him to.

Ask and you will receive, seek and you will find, knock and the door shall be opened unto you. (Matthew 7:7)

When I was twelve years old, I had many talents and abilities. I would run track and every meet I had I experienced victory because I prayed before every race. Another talent I had was sewing. No one ever taught me how to sew and I never owned a sewing machine. With just a needle and thread I was able to turn old clothing into something professional. The power of prayer increased my skills and abilities. At twelve I learned that God is real. He answers me when I pray to Him. As a born-again Christian for twenty-six years, I have no doubt in my mind that prayer must be the foundation between me, you, and God.

The More I Pray

To maintain your new life with Christ you must develop a prayerful lifestyle which will produce a powerful dynamic relationship of love, humility, unity, intimacy, and Spirituality for the good of our salvation both now and forever.

If ye abide in me, and my words abide in you, ye shall ask what ye will, and it shall be done unto you. Amen.
John 15:7

Chapter One

What Really is Prayer?

Remember what I told you about me reading my Bible as a child. You too need to begin reading your Bible as a child of God. Whether you are young or old it really does not matter who you are you must indulge in taking up the Bible and reading it. Why? Because, when you read your Bible it makes you want to pray, and it teaches you how to pray (talk to God). Did you know that the words written in the Bible is not only about God, but it is God Himself speaking to you? What do you do when someone is talking to you? Don't you let them talk while you listen? When it's your time to talk they listen, so it is with God. He speaks to you and you speak back to Him that is called prayer, it's talking to God in a communicating manner. Why is it necessary to read your Bible? To develop a prayerful lifestyle, you must use the Word of God to lay the foundation when you pray. Then your prayer life will receive attention from God. He knows and understands His own language. When you read, study, meditate, communicate, discuss or reason and witness to someone, your faith in God continues to grow. Your love, hope, trust, peace, and patients are the fruits of the Spirit. Joy, long-suffering and the blessing of God will rest upon you. Your prayer life will be a powerful testimony to others.

But without faith it is impossible to please God, for he that cometh to God must believe that he is, and that he is a rewarder of them that diligently seek Him.

Hebrews 11:6

The More I Pray

Prayer is not just talking to God and presenting Him with a "Give me list" or "I Want this and that now request." Even though asking is a must:

Ask and you shall receive, seek and you will find, knock and the door shall be opened onto you.

Matthew 7:7

BUT it should not be the beginning of your prayer. Prayer is a natural resource given to mankind by God through which we can communicate one on one with the one who created everything in this world including us. The purpose of prayer is to create a loving and a lasting personal relationship with God not only in this world but for eternity. Just like God provides air to our lungs. Air is essential for breathing. It keeps us alive. He expects us to maintain our relationship with Him through daily prayers. No wonder Jesus said:

Man ought always to pray and not faint. (discourage)

Luke 18:1

If you are not praying, you are fainting. If you are not breathing, you are dead. Praying keeps you alive and well up to date with what God is saying and doing during every season of our lives while here on earth and until He comes back to take us with Him. Prayer is designed by God Himself. It is the Spiritual connector between God and man and it produces a solid personal relationship with Him. It holds us together in unity as like a Father and son relationship. Prayer changes the heart and mindset of any individual who decides to pray willingly, regularly, unconditionally, correctly, collectively, and personally.

Prayer is the key to building a perfect relationship with God, our Father. Praying is simple yet, powerful and is

The More I Pray

recognized as the sinner's prayer because sinners can be converted into saints. That is why prayer is the first key of many to be used. It has incredible, dynamics and transforming power to change us from the inside out. Prayer penetrates the hardest places of life. It sends a ray of light into the darkest places. Because of prayer situations that are dead come alive and yokes are destroyed.

> **For his anger endureth but a moment: in his favour is life: weeping may endure for a night but, joy cometh in the morning.**
> **Psalm 30:5**

Burdens are removed, and joy comes when you pray. Prayer is a divine instrument used to love our enemies. If not for prayer, we would never get a chance to love our enemies.

> **But I say unto you, love your enemies, bless them that curse you, do good to them that hate you, and pray for them that despitefully use you",**
> **Matthew 5:44**

We can love our enemies by praying for them.

> **For if ye love them which love you, what reward have ye? do not even the publicans the same?**
> **Matthew 5:46**

Prayer is a divine opportunity which God has given to mankind. The most valuable resource which allows us access to the throne of God to speak to the King of Kings and the Lord of Lords. That's why God created us in His image and His likeness to relate, converse, communicate, and to intimate Him. Real prayers put us into to ships. They

The More I Pray

are worship, fellowship, partnership, membership, friendship, relationship, and the lordship of Christ Jesus. God gets to exercise his lordship over us when we spend quality time with Him. He is the one whom we love the most. It lets us know our heart towards Him and His heart towards us. It's like getting to know each other and growing closer forever and ever. That's the power of prayer. Prayer takes us into the presence of God, and He releases His power in us through the Holy Spirit. This is how we receive a transformation of our minds in our spirit, soul, and body. The Holy Spirit also helps us to change our attitudes and gives us the power to deal with circumstances, situations, conditions, problems, trials, and troubles that we constantly must face when the devil attacks us. Prayer changes things. It shines the light on dark places of our lives so that we can see. Prayer exposes Satan's secret weapons that he uses to deceive God's chosen people because he has years of experience in sin. Satan has major strategies! We cannot stand up to Him unless we become Prayer-Warriors in Jesus' name. Also, when we pray, we receive strength, insight, secret information, divine revelation, divine impartation, wisdom, knowledge, and understanding from God. Prayer cannot be effectually, fervently, or relatively communicated to God if we do not read and study His Word daily. It's imperative that we meditate on it in your hearts and keep it in your minds.

> **Study to show thyself approved unto God, a workman that needeth not to be ashamed, rightly dividing the word of truth.**
>
> **2 Timothy 2:15**

You cannot build a strong relationship with God without His Word.

The More I Pray

God honors His Word above His name.

In the beginning was the Word, and the Word was with God, and the Word was God.

John 1:1

Prayer must have these implications:
- The giving of yourself
- surrendering your will
- emotions
- humbling of yourself
- the asking for forgiveness
- repenting from your sins
- forgiving those who've done you wrong

For if ye forgive men their trespasses, your heavenly Father will also forgive you:

Matthew 6:14

Remove hatred that is in your heart. Along with malice, jealousy, envy, moods, attitudes, meanness, greediness, funniness, hypocrisy, deceitfulness, laziness, selfishness and business.

If my people, which are called by my name, shall humble themselves, and pray, and seek my face, and turn from their wicked ways: then will I hear from heaven, and will forgive their sin, and will heal their land.

2 Chronicles 7:14

Pray with the understanding that this is the divine way to approach the throne of God. Fast, read the scriptures, be

The More I Pray

prepared in the Spirit of your mind. Find a place in your home and make it a Holy place. Chose a position for yourself alone or with loved ones and other family members. Set aside a special time, clear the atmosphere, and let there be peace. Put aside pride and arrogance, become like a little child and be simple and humble. Make a strong effort and give attention to God. Know that God, whom you're praying to rules and rains over the entire earth. He is God over all and there is none like Him. Reverence Him! He owns the air that we breathe! His very presence keeps you alive! Give Him:

1. Worship
2. Praise and thanks
3. Glory and honor
4. Exaltation
5. Magnify Him
6. Love Him
7. Make your request known unto Him.
8. Be obedient to Him

Make a joyful noise unto the LORD, all ye lands. Serve the LORD with gladness: come before his presence with singing. Know ye that the LORD he is God: it is he that hath made us, and not we ourselves: we are his people, and the sheep of his pasture. Enter into his gates with thanksgiving, and into his courts with praise be thankful unto him and bless his name. For the LORD is good: his mercy is everlasting: and his truth endureth to all generations.

Psalm 100:1-5

Laziness is one of the main reasons why we as believers do not receive answers to our prayers. We are lazy

The More I Pray

in applying divine principles that will produce the right results. We do not want to spend time with God, instead, we are in a hurry and we only want what He has in His hands. Prayer is not just coming to God because you need something. It is not an alternative or a substitute. Prayer ought to be a way of life. It should encompass fasting and obeying. I often hear Christians say, "Well! I have nothing else to do but pray! I have tried everything, and nothing seems to work so, I guess I'll just pray." People say things like, "I don't have time to pray every day. Maybe when I have time, I will." Don't wait until you have a need, or you're faced with a terrible situation to praise God. This should be done as often as you breathe! Prayer proves your faith and reminds you as to why you are alive. It is a powerful principle that needs to be applied to our daily practice of living.

> **For in him we live, and move, and have our being: as certain also of your own poets have said, for we are also his offspring.**
> **Acts 17:28**

Before Jesus came on the scene, the men of old, servants and prophets prayed. When God called Abram out of his homeland to go to the land of Canaan.

> **And Abram built an altar and prayed.**
> **Genesis 12:8**

As he continued his journey he worshiped, prayed, called upon the name of the Lord, and gave thanks each step of the way.

> **And Noah built an altar unto the Lord and prayed and took from every clean beast and offered a sacrifice as an offering.**

The More I Pray

Genesis 8:20

And the Lord smelled a sweet savor and the Lord said in his heart I will not curse the ground anymore for man sake.
Genesis 8:21

God made a promise to Himself that He will not destroy evil mankind as He did in the flood all because one just man prayed and gave an offering as a sacrifice. God turned around and gave the entire world a second chance. God blessed Noah and his sons and said unto them:

Be fruitful, multiply and replenish the earth.
Genesis 1:28

Pray with the understanding in the Old Testament, when the old prayed to God, He answered with signs, wonders, and miracles. Their prayers reached the heart of God because they prayed from their hearts. They knew that God is a Spirit and those who worship Him (live for Him) must worship in Spirit and in Truth (John 4:24). They woke up early in the morning to call upon God, then He spoke back to them and they did as He said. They were obedient to his voice. When we are faced with an overwhelming problem this is how we react. "I don't know why God is not answering my prayers, I have been attending church every Sunday, giving my tithes and offerings, I participate in all church activities, I serve on the Deacon Board, I sing in the choir, I served as an usher, I'm on the prayer team, and I have memorized scriptures but, things seem to be getting worst! God, where are you? When will you show up? This is not working out!" Just listen to yourself. Prayer must come from a heart of love, not from your head and according to all

The More I Pray

you are thinking or doing. Prayer is not complaining to God; it's not telling God you're disappointed in Him or how much you did for Him and how much He has not lived up to our expectations. After all, we have done? Let's be honest. God never planned to provide for us according to how many things we did for Him. We are not working to impress Him.

This book of the law shall not depart out of thy mouth but thou shalt meditate therein day and night that thou mayest observe to do according to all that is written therein, for then thou wilt make your own way prosperous and then you should have good success.

Joshua 1:8

Be careful for nothing: but in everything by prayer and supplication with thanksgiving let your requests be made known unto God. And the peace of God which passeth all understanding shall keep your heart and minds through Christ Jesus.

Philippians 4:6,7

Prayer is a channel through which we can receive peace of mind and a heart that's kept in the Word of God through Christ.

Jesus said unto Him, thou shalt love the Lord thy God with all thy heart, and with all thy soul, and all thy mind, this is the first and great commandment. And the second is like unto it, thou shalt love thy neighbor as thyself.

Matthew 22:37-39

What does love have to do with prayer? I am glad you asked! Prayer is more than just words repeated and recited in the ears of God. You must remember to whom you are addressing. He is God, creator of heaven, earth and

The More I Pray

everything else. You are not praying to the Statue of Liberty, a historical figure or a monument. He is God the Father, Maker and Creator. He rules in the affairs of men. He cares, hears, and answers. He is not a figment of your imagination. He is REAL! King of Kings and Lord of Lords. He reigns over all. He is almighty, all powerful, omnipotent, omniscient, and omnipresent. His very name means supernatural. Prayer is not man's idea, it's God's ideal method for Him to meet us at our point of need. But it is our responsibility to pray. Ask, seek, and knock! The people of old were servants of God. We need to come back to that place of serving and spend time in God's presence in prayer.

Abram, Moses, Elijah, Jacob, Isaac, David, and Daniel all prayed three times a day, fasted on a regular basis, and they listened and waited to hear the voice of God. They all moved according to instruction and directions. They gave thanks and praise, and this touched the heart of God. Then God responded as they waited patiently in obedience with expectation. Prayer produces the strength to make strong every foundation that is set for believers to build their life upon. Prayer strengthens the cord that binds families together in God's love. Mother's need it, Father 's needs it, wives, husbands, sons and daughters (all families need God's love). Therefore, all families need to pray. Jackie DeShannon sang a song that declared, "What the world needs now is love." Afterward, Tina Turner sang the question, "What's love got to do with it?" EVERYTHING! Everything good and right is built on God's love!

For God so loved the world that he gave his only begotten son that whosoever believeth in Him should not perish but have eternal life."

John 3:16

If it wasn't for prayer, we would not be able to pass on God's love to others. Prayer is a Spiritual vehicle that we

The More I Pray

use to transport love to one another. No prayer, no power, no love! A prayerless generation is a powerless generation and a loveless generation. Think about how much power we have given to the devil by removing prayer for homes, schools, government offices, courthouses, and The White House. We have forgotten the God who made it possible for us to have everything we have.

Love never fails and love conquers all.
1 Corinthians 13:8

Therefore, we must pray with understanding, so that our prayers could be answered. If love never fails, then prayer never fails and if love conquers all then, prayer conquers all. I could still hear some Christians say, "I am waiting on God" but, I can also hear God say, "I am waiting on you to pray the right words, pray with the right heart, with the right attitude, and with understanding."

I am your servant, give me understanding that I may know your testimonies.
Psalm 119:125

Chapter Two

Jesus Healed, Teaching And Preaching Ministry

Jesus had just come out of the Jordan River after being baptized by John the Baptist. He was approved by God when the voice came from heaven, "This is my beloved Son in whom I am well pleased." Afterward, He was led by the Spirit and was tempted by the devil. When he passed all His tests, the angels came and ministered unto Him. He then went out immediately and selected his followers who were the twelve disciples and began preaching and teaching the gospel of the Kingdom of God and healing all manner of diseases. Multitudes of people begin following Him and his fame spread throughout Galilee and Jerusalem (read Matthew chapter 13 and Matthew 4:1-22). The people followed Jesus everywhere He went with His disciples, He knew who He was and what He was born to do. He knew God was His Father and He Jesus was His Son. He understood His mission here on earth, He knew God's will for His life and He knew He had to go to the cross to be crucified for the sins of mankind. He knew He would be raised the third day from the dead and returned to Heaven where He came from. To sit at the right hand of God His Father, to pray and intercede daily for us whom He has chosen. Jesus begins His ministry on earth by being a perfect example of everything his Father sent Him to do.

For I came down from heaven not to do my own will, but the will of Him that sent me.

John 6:38

The More I Pray

And there followed Him great multitudes of people from Galilee and from Decapolis and from Jerusalem and from Judea and from beyond Jordan.

Matthew 4:25

And seeing the multitudes, he went up into a mountain: and when he was set, his disciples came unto him: And he opened his mouth, and taught them, saying, Blessed are the poor in spirit: for theirs is the kingdom of heaven.

Matthew 5:1-3

Read Matthew 5:3 about the be attitudes.

Jesus said rejoice and be exceeding glad for great is your reward in heaven for so persecuted they the prophets which were before you.

Matthew 5:12

Jesus taught multitudes of people along with His disciples about a time where they would be persecuted for following Him. They should not be sad nor discouraged and turn back, because God would reward them for their faithfulness in learning the truth, practicing truth, and telling others about the Good News as they traveled. Jesus taught them that they were the salt of the earth. (Matthew 5:13) He taught about being the light of the world. (Matthew 5:14) and how they should shine for the entire world to see the power of the Holy Spirit working in them. It was imperative to pray, teach others and celebrate as the people began to glorify God who is in Heaven.

Think not that I am come to destroy the law or the profits, I am not come to destroy, but to fulfill."

Matthew 5:17

The More I Pray

Jesus taught the people and His disciples that they had a choice. They could continue practicing their religious customs or they could choose to receive the truth about the Gospel of Christ Jesus, who would change their old ways of thinking. Instead, of praying the way the Scribes and the Pharisees did they could choose to have a relationship with God the Father, by receiving the Word of truth in their hearts. Being a hearer or a teller of the truth and not being a doer of it wasn't good enough. They must've practiced, preached, and lived the truth being living examples to their fellow believers.

This is what Jesus taught his followers, that except your righteousness exceeds the righteousness of the religious people, he shall in no case enter into the kingdom of Heaven."

Matthew 5:20

Jesus knew the religious people believed they were righteous because they prayed using many words, spoke loudly, tore their clothes, fasted many days, offered sacrifices, looked, dressed and walked Holy. They spent time in the Holy temple made with hands. Jesus wants us to know as Christian believers that in this day and time. This is the same lessons he taught them. Man looks at the outward appearance and God looks on the Heart (1 Samuel 16:7). Well! What does all of this have to do with prayer? I am glad you asked. If you know what you believe, what you have to do and how to do it, when and why you should do what you believe, then you know the truth and you will practice the truth daily. Our prayers will be heard by God. The Father will answer in His time according to His Word. God hears and answer prayers when it is directed to Him. It's important that you know who you are in Christ Jesus. You are no longer a religious creature; you are a new creature in Christ.

The More I Pray

"therefore, if any man be in Christ, he is a new creature, all things are passed away behold all things become new."

2 Corinthians 5:17

Jesus taught the people to love their enemies which is quite the opposite to the old saying

"an eye for an eye and a tooth for a tooth."

Matthew 5:38

"but I say (Jesus speaking) Love your enemies, bless them that curse you, do good to those that hate and pray for them which despitefully use you and persecute you."

Matthew 5:44

Jesus knew that people would attack those who follow His teachings, preaching and respected His healing power.

"Jesus said, and ye shall be hated of all men for my name sake, but he that endureth to the end shall be saved."

Matthew 10:22

"Be ye therefore perfect even as your heavenly Father which is in heaven is perfect."

Matthew 5:48

"and Jesus went above all Galilee teaching in their synagogues and preaching the gospel of the kingdom and

healing all manner of sicknesses and disease among the people."

Matthew 4:23

The More I Pray

Chapter Three
Jesus Taught His Disciples How to Pray

"After this manner therefore pray ye: Our Father which art in heaven, Hallowed be thy name. Thy kingdom come, Thy will be done in earth, as it is in heaven. us this day our daily bread. And forgive us our debts, as we forgive our debtors. And lead us not into temptation but deliver us from evil: For thine is the kingdom, and the power, and the glory, forever. Amen."

Matthew 6:9

The disciples asked Jesus to teach them how to pray. It is important for us Christian believers to learn how to pray. To many of God's people are still struggling with unanswered prayers, all because we have not been taught how to pray. We have settled where we are in our walk with God. We are stuck in the box, worrying, complaining, murmuring, and NOT praying, simply because we say we don't know what else to pray for. While God is saying we have not even prayed yet.

James said, **"If any of you lack wisdom, let him ask of God, that giveth to all men liberally, and upbraideth not:and it shall be given him. But let him ask in faith, nothing wavering. For he that wavereth is like a wave of the sea driven with the wind and tossed. For let not that man think that he shall receive any thing of the Lord. A double minded man is unstable in all his ways."**

James 1:5-8

The More I Pray

"be ye therefore perfect even as your heavenly Father, which is in Heaven is perfect."

Matthew 5:48

We have a little problem here. Or should I say, "big one!" Christians everywhere are still saying "I can't be perfect because I am human." If Jesus says we can be perfect than we can. We have the perfect one living in us,

"Greater is he that is in me than he that is in the world."

1 John 4:4

Jesus knew when He would return to Heaven where He came from and the disciples were to finish his ministry for his Kingdom the way he did. That is why he said, **"Greater works than these will you do because I go to my Father" (John 14:12).**

He also knew that the disciples had to be divinely connected to the Father and Spiritual orientated to do greater works. They had to receive wisdom and apply it to their prayer lives, to work the works He sent them to do. We too as Christian believers need to follow Jesus and become His disciples in the world we live in today. Where wars and rumors of wars, crimes, violence, immorality, pornography, heresy, so much sexual perversion, and abominable lifestyle have taken over our society, our homes, schools, government houses, and even in some of our churches. There isn't a day without these events happening so there should not be a day without prayer in our Christian homes. We must learn to pray effectively. Jesus taught his disciples how to pray, He knew they would face obstacles, opposition and challenges that were before them. Especially, from the Roman government and other religious leaders, just like they were

The More I Pray

terribly against Jesus' teaching, preaching, and healing ministry

"Jesus had to prepare the disciples, they had to be strengthened through their prayers to use their faith to win against the enemy."

Matthew 10:22

As Christians we too in this day and time are faced with great and evil oppositions, challenges and obstacles daily increasing in our world. We too need to pray like Jesus did and like he taught his disciples to pray. Pray with the Understanding Remember what James said in James 1:5-8 why we need to learn how to pray. Well! James said something else

"Ye lust, and have not, ye kill and desire to have and cannot obtain, ye fight and war, yet we have not because ye ask not, because ye ask amiss, that ye may consume it upon your own lust. ye adulterers and adulterous know ye not that friendship of the world is enmity with God? Whosoever therefore will be a friend of the world is an enemy of God. Submit yourself therefore to God, resist the devil and he will flee from you. Draw nigh to God and he will draw nigh to you."

James 4:2-8

How would we be able to do what James said if we do not know how to pray? Praying the way Jesus taught His disciples would prepare us to relatively communicate our prayers to God the Father. With prayer we would be able to pray God's Word and not just vain empty words that are meaningless. Jesus desires for us to develop the kind of character He has just as Paul and Silas, James, John, and Peter. These followed the divine principles, orders, methods,

The More I Pray

and walked in the very footsteps that Jesus designed for them to continue the mission He started.

"Then the eleven disciples went away into Galilee, unto a mountain where Jesus had appointed them and when they saw Him they worshipped Him, but some doubted and Jesus came and spake unto to them saying all power is given unto me in Heaven and in earth, go ye therefore and teach all nations, baptizing them in the name of the Father, and of the Son, and of the Holy Ghost. Teaching them to observe all things I have commanded you, and lo, I am with you always, even unto the end of the world."
Matthew 28:16-20

Jesus is God and it is He who gives this command recognized as *The Great Commission* to the eleven. He also gave them power to carry out the mission, preaching, teaching, healing this sick, and delivering those held in bondage to customs, traditions and religion. The reason why we as followers need to know how to pray is because God does not do anything by chance or by accident. God is a God of divine order, purpose, plan, principles, instructions, design, destiny, and possibility. Everything He does will always have a good ending. He wants us to receive answers to our prayers but, we must pray as Jesus says. Here we go!

"And when thou prayest don't be like the hypocrites are, for they love to pray standing in the synagogues and in the corners of the streets that they may be heard by others, verily verily I say unto you they have their reward."
Matthew 6:5

These are some of the instructions,

The More I Pray

"but when you pray use not vain repetitions as the heathens do. For they think they should be heard for their much speaking."

Matthew 6:7

This is what He means, do not pray because you want to be seen or heard by others. Prayer is not a recitation or a poem. It is not a religious practice. Nor is it just a family tradition. Could it be some words put together and speak when you get into trouble and want to get out? It is not just a church thing or a Christian duty. Prayer is real. God first used prayer in Genesis 1:3. He stated, "Let there be light." This was God's first prayer to Himself. He spoke by faith and with designated power in his spoken words, it was manifested and there was light. His prayer produced supernatural and powerful results. It's okay to pray in secret. Find a place in your home where you can shut yourself in with the Father. Pray one on one every day in prayer. Close the door. Become private and personal with Him. Have your Bible with you? Invite the Holy Spirit into your room. Read and study. Pray to the Father in Jesus' name, meditate on some of the scriptures and let the Holy Spirit have His way in you. Prayer must begin with you first, alone with God. Practice His presence. Prayer must be practiced in secret first. God is Holy and He desires a Holy people to dwell in a Holy place.

"But when thou prayest, enter thy closet and when thou hast shut thy door, pray to thine Father which is in secret, and thy Father who seeth in secret will reward you openly."

Matthew 6:6

I have found this to be very true based on my own experiences in answered prayer. Prayer should be first in your heart, in your home, then in your family, and then continue from there. Receive this revelation on how to pray and you will receive victory in your prayer life

The More I Pray

Chapter Four

Is There a Right Way to Pray?

And Jesus spake this parable unto certain which trusted in themselves that they were righteous and despised others he says two men went into the temple to pray the one a pharisee and the other a publican the pharisee stood and prayed this thus with Himself God I thank thee that I am not like other men are extortioners unjust adulterers or even as the publican I fast twice in the week I give tithes all I possess And the publican standing a far off would not lift so much as his eyes unto heaven but smote upon his breast saying God be merciful to me a sinner I tell you this man went down to his house justified rather than The other For everyone who exalteth Himself shall be abased and he that humbleth Himself shall be exalted.

Luke 18:9-14

For whosoever exalteth himself shall be abased: and he that humbleth himself shall be exalted.

Luke 14:11

In this, the Pharisee represents religious prayer and the publican represents a person who is humble. He realized that he is a sinner and needed forgiveness for his sins so he can begin his new relationship with the Father

For all have sinned and come short of the glory of God.

Romans 3:23

The More I Pray

If my people, which are called by my name, shall humble themselves, and pray, and seek my face, and turn from their wicked ways: then will I hear from heaven, and will forgive their sin, and will heal their land.

2 Chronicles 7:14

This is extremely necessary for us as God's people to know there is a right way to pray. If you want your prayers to be answered in God's time and God's way and according to God's Word and His will then we must follow His directions. These are some of the things you need to understand. Remember, you must pray with understanding according to 2 Chronicles 7:14. Certain conditions must be met before you receive answers to your prayers. As a Christian, you first must have a relationship with the Father as a child of God through Jesus Christ. We must bear His name also.

And you hath he quickened, who were dead in trespasses and sins; Wherein in time past ye walked according to the course of this world, according to the prince of the power of the air, the spirit that now worketh in the children of disobedience: Among whom also we all had our conversation in times past in the lusts of our flesh, fulfilling the desires of the flesh and of the mind; and were by nature the children of wrath, even as others.

Ephesians 2:1-6

There are too many of us Christians who do not know what the scriptures say about how to pray. We are praying in ignorance (not knowing). Pay attention to what the book of Ephesians 2 teaches us. We are no longer children of the

The More I Pray

world or children of disobedience. We are now children of the light and only of the living God. God who is rich in mercy and His great love is indescribable. He loves us even when we were dead in sin. By grace, we are saved. It is He who has raised us up together and made us sit together in heavenly places in Christ Jesus.

It is important that you know who you are. We are the people who are called by His name. We have been given our position of authority in Christ Jesus to pray uncompromising prayers 2nd Chronicles 7:14 says, " If my people, which are called by my name, shall humble themselves, and pray, and seek my face, and turn from their wicked ways; then will I hear from heaven, and will forgive their sin, and will heal their land." This is my question to us as God's people. Do we understand that the right way to pray begins with obedience and our prayer depends on the relationship we have with the Father answers? God has made lots of promises in His Word to His chosen people and He has kept them all. He has made a covenant with us that He has never broken. All because He is a promise keeper.

God is not a man, that he should lie; neither the son of man, that he should repentant he said, and shall he not do it? or hath he spoken, and shall he not make it good?

Numbers 23:19

He hath blessed and I cannot reverse it Amen! It is time for Christians to wake up from their sleep, slumber and take hold of the scriptures. Find out what is in them for us. We are chosen by God. We have been drafted in and have equal rights to His promises. Just as to Abraham, to Isaac

The More I Pray

and Jacob and now we have a better covenant. We are joint heirs with Christ Jesus. He became the sacrifice for our sins and we are now redeemed by His shed blood, Jesus is seated at the right hand of God the Father. He is interceding and praying daily for us. We are seated with Him in Heavenly places. All the promises that God has made are yes and Amen. We can only access these promises through our prayers. God's love for us is unconditional but, every promise comes with conditions and prayer is the foundation for these conditions being met., Just like God used Moses as a mediator to stand between God and the people to deliver His chosen people from Egypt's bondage. They were a people who did not know God but, He chose Moses to deliver them. Moses became the intercessor and prayed to God for the people. It was through his effectual fervent prayer that allowed Him to see God face to face. With that God was able to use Him as a deliverer. Moses led the slaves into the wilderness where they could serve God for themselves and experience His supernatural power. God performed miracles, signs, and wonder. (Deuteronomy 34:10) God knew Moses and Moses knew Him. Many of God's people do not receive their blessing because they do not know God face to face. They are not aware of the promises written in scriptures. They do not know who they are and who Jesus is.   They do not have a covenant relationship with the Father, Son, and the Holy Spirit. However, we want God to hear us when we pray concerning all the things we need. When the daily circumstances of life try to overtake us and the problems of life invade our Spiritual territories, we need our Father's help because there is so much going on in our thoughts and minds that it's only the Word that rest in our hearts will help.

The More I Pray

Thy word have I hid in my heart that I might not sin against thee.

Psalm 119:11

The world is slowly crumbling, and believers only have the Word to stand on. Our lives are useless without the Word of God being a part of the foundation. We have it. Use it! You will be shocked to find out how little of the Word we hide in our hearts. We carry the Word in very small portions. We put it on a shelf and pull it out only when it's convenient. We call ourselves Christians but, don't always live by the Word. Preposterous! We go to the church house every Sunday. We sing, shout and say Amen. We pray only when in trouble and sometimes loudly in a prayer meeting.

If you remain in me and my words remain in you, ask whatever you wish, and it will be done for you.

John 15:7

This is what Jesus said to His disciples and He is still saying this to us now, "Do not be like the heathens. They are just a bunch of religious people who are self-righteous. They begin their prayers by letting God know how good they have been and that is why He should answer their prayers. Do we know before we build a relation, we ought to lay a foundation first (John 15:7)? We must spend quality time with our Father praying, praising, worshiping and giving our tithes and offerings. We should live holy in secret, forgive,

The More I Pray

have love one for another, read, study, meditate, obey the word and have faith in God. It is important that we die daily to self (humility) and love God (Matthew 22:37). Do you remember the parable about the two men who went up to pray? The Pharisee prayed to himself, but the publican prayed with a humble and truthful heart, acknowledging God for who He is, and reverencing Him in his prayer. Jesus wants us to pray the right way. Not only to get our prayers answered but, He wants us to enter a personal intimate relationship with the Father through the Son and the Holy Spirit. This will develop the Jesus character within us so that we can be in touch with our victory.

Praying correctly means praying righteously and not religiously. Praying should not be traditional or empty words, instead, power should be added by remembering Jesus's promises and remember who you are addressing. Praying correctly means doing so with a heart to heart communication with Jesus, our perfect example, He is our mediator and intercessor. He knows how to pray Himself! He prayed to His Father. He's One who prays, he is Supernatural, the Beginning and the End, Alpha and Omega. God our Father has given us a divine prayer pattern to follow.

"And when you pray, do not be like the hypocrites, for they love to pray standing in the synagogues and on the street corners to be seen by others. Truly I tell you, they have received their reward in full. 6 But when you pray, go into your room, close the door and pray to your Father, who is unseen. Then your Father, who sees what is done in secret, will reward you. And when you pray, do not keep on babbling like pagans, for they think they will be heard because of their many words. Do not be like them, for your Father knows what you need before you ask him. "This, then, is how you should pray:" 'Our

The More I Pray

Father in heaven, hallowed be your name, your kingdom come, your will be done, on earth as it is in heaven. Give us today our daily bread. And forgive us our debts, as we also have forgiven our debtors. lead us not into temptation but deliver us from the evil one.

Matthew 6: 5-13

Chapter Five
Pray To The Father In Jesus' Name!

Then cometh Jesus with them unto a place called gethsemane, and saith unto the disciples, sit ye here while I go yonder."

Matthew 26:36

"And he went a little farther, and fell on his face and prayed, O my Father if it be possible let this cup be pass from me, nevertheless not as I will but as thou wilt.

Matthew 26:39

Remember, I told you Jesus knows how to pray. He is our perfect example to follow. First, He is in a place alone, in the presence of His Father. Then, He fell on His face which is a humble position to seek God's strength, wisdom, knowledge, understanding, instruction and direction, He then prayed. He opened His mouth and spoke to His Father. Listen how He began His prayer. **"Oh, my Father!"** Jesus knew He was the Son and God who is His Father. He knew this His approach was in Divine order. He proceeded in His prayer by letting the Father know that it's not about what He wanted for Himself but, His desire was to His Father s will be supreme to His own. Note this. Even though Jesus knew who He was and what He came to earth to do, He prayed to His Father. He recognized that He was 100% human and His five senses were at work. Yet, He was 100% God. He had both the flesh side and God Side. He could not bear the pain and suffering through the crucifixion process in His flesh unless His Father gave Him the strength to endure the agony on the cross until His mission was accomplished. He had to be prepared and ready Spiritually by the one who sent Him

The More I Pray

to earth. He had to pray for the Holy Spirit to help Him. The Holy Spirit is God's Spirit in Jesus' manifesting the greatness of God's unconditional love for mankind.

For God so love the world that he gave his only begotten son that whosoever believeth in Him should not perish but have eternal life."

John 3:16

As Christians, we must learn to pray right. Through righteous prayers, we are able to get God's attention and His response. Do you realize that we are Jesus disciples and the prayer patterns given is exactly what is written in 2 Chronicles 7:14. Look at the scriptures in the Old Testament.

If my people, who are called by my name, will humble themselves and pray and seek my face and turn from their wicked ways, then I will hear from heaven, and I will forgive their sin and will heal their land.

2 Chronicles 7:14

Jesus is instructing us to pray the same way God inspired the prophets of old to pray. From the beginning Jesus was God. To obtain answers to prayers, humbleness and obedience is required.

Step One. **"Our Father which art in heaven, Hallowed be thy name."**

Begin your prayer with acknowledgement that God is your Father and you are His child. He cares about your total wellbeing. Let Him know that you are totally depending on Him as His child. Keep in mind that you are not talking to your earthly Father but, to your Heavenly Father. He is

The More I Pray

the one who is over all. He loves you and cares for you more than your mother, father, friends, and family. He loves you more than yourself. He saved you from your sins (John 3:16). Understand that He is yours and you are His. Know that He is not just a figment of our imagination or an idol nor a statue, He is REAL! He created the world and everything in it (Psalm 24).

Matthew 6:6 says, "Pray to the Father which is in secret and thy Father which sees in secret will reward thee openly."

God, the Father has eyes and He sees you even though you cannot see Him. He has ears and He hear you. You can hear Him when He speaks to you. If you listen for His voice. If you study his word with readiness. Pray! He knows everything you need before you even ask. He owns EVERYTHING you would ever need.

The earth is the lord and the fullness thereof: the world and everything there in."

Psalm 24:1

Don't be afraid to ask Him for anything, he said "ask what you will, and it shall be done unto you.

Matthew 7:7

But there are conditions to be met.

"if you abide in me and my words abide in you, you shall ask what you will, and it shall be done unto you."

John 15:7

When you learn how much your Father owns, who He really is and how much you can become like Him, you

The More I Pray

can have that He possesses. (Matthew 22:37) Jesus said to the lawyer who asked Him which is the greatest commandment? Jesus said unto Him "Thou shalt love the lord with all thine heart, soul and mind and love thy neighbor as yourself." How you approach Him in your prayer time matters. Psalm 100:1-5, says "Make a joyful noise unto the Lord all ye lands, serve the Lord with gladness, come before His presence with singing. Know ye that the lord he is God. It is he that made us and not we ourselves. We are his people and the sheep of his pasture. Enter his gates with thanksgiving and into his courts with praise. Be thankful unto Him and bless his holy name. For the lord is good and his mercy is everlasting. And his truth endureth to all generations."

Don't be afraid to tell Him you love Him with all your heart. God doesn't want us to come before Him with a "give me" list. We should not be beggars nor strangers, but we are children of the most high God and He is our Father. He loves us!

How do people spend their time together when they are in a love relationship? How do they get to know one another? By enjoying the presence of each other, finding out differences and similarities in one another's lives. The motive is always to get closer. As children of God and Christian believers, let's pray with understanding. That is exactly what our Father wants for us. He wants us to build a closer relationship with Him so He can hear and answer our prayers, building a heart to heart connection that will last for eternity. Think about the world we live in today. Father s, sons, mothers and daughters, and families disagree. Children are being neglected and rejected increasingly in our homes and neighborhoods all around the world. That's why we need our Heavenly Father in our home (heart) and everywhere we go. He will be with us.

The More I Pray

"When my mother and my Father forsake me, the Lord will take me up."

Psalms 27:10

"Hallowed be thy name." (Matthew 6:9) Pray in Jesus' name. The name Jesus is sacred, consecrated and holy. Begin your prayer by adding the name Jesus to it. God has given us a name that is above every other name. In John 14:16, Jesus said to Thomas who was one of his disciples, " **I am the way the truth and the light no man cometh unto the Father but by me."** Our prayers reached the Father when we say, "In the name of Jesus" or "in Jesus' name." Jesus is the mediator between God and man. Pray in the name of Jesus because He is the Word who became flesh and dwelt amongst us. He is the one who paid the sacrifice for all sins when He died on the cross. He shed His blood. He paid the price for sins He never committed. He is God's only begotten Son. He came from His Father to earth to show us the right way. He performed miracles in the lives of many people. During His time here on earth, He turned water into wine, opened the eyes of the blind, rebuked the wind and the ways and they obeyed Him. He walked on water, ascended back to Heaven where He is seated at the right hand of God the Father. This making intercession for us who the Father has chosen before the foundation of the world. His name is Jesus. He is from the beginning. He was, he is, and He is to come (Revelation 1:5-8) Jesus Christ, the faithful witness and the first begotten of the dead! The Prince of the kings of the earth unto Him that loved us. It was He who washed us from our sins in His own blood (John 10:27- 30). My sheep hear my voice and I know them and they follow me (28) and I give unto them eternal life and they shall not perish neither shall man pluck them out from my hand (29) my Father which gave them to me is greater is greater than all, and no man is able to pluck them from my Father 's hand (30) it and the Father are one. Believe me when I say there is power in

The More I Pray

the name of Jesus, to break every chain that seem to bind you. If you will ask in Jesus' name, there is forgiveness of sins in the in the name of Jesus. If you will confess your sins, He is faithful and just to forgive and cleanse from all unrighteousness (1 John 1:9).

There is:

- Salvation
- Deliverance
- Freedom
- Wisdom
- Healing
- Peace
- Love
- Joy
- Obedience
- Answers to prayers
- Solutions to problems
- Transformation
- Restoration
- Wholeness
- Holiness
- Wisdom
- Knowledge
- Understanding
- Revelation
- Inspiration
- Information
- Education
- Impartation
- Secret information
- and so much more

We can go on and on. Miracles, signs and wonders takes place when we pray in Jesus' name. Oh, the name of Jesus kings and kingdoms shall all pass away but there is something about that name "The name of the LORD is a strong tower: the righteous runneth into it and is safe (Proverbs 18:10).

"That at the name of Jesus every knee should bow, of things in heaven, and things in earth, and things under the earth; Philippians 2:10). Sinners are saved in the name of Jesus. Demons tremble at His name. Every tongue will acknowledge that Jesus Christ is Lord due to His name. Evil forces are driven out in the name of Jesus. It's the sweetest name on earth. J for Jesus, E for eternity, S for Savior, U for unity and S for the Son of God. When we pray in Jesus' name, we are becoming like Him. God is our Father. He made many promises in His Word to those who are His children.

We have a new and better covenant with Jesus because of His bloodshed also. Now we can have a personal relationship through Jesus our Savior and Lord. Only He is our sacrifice for sins. He's our Redeemer, our High Priest, and the Mediator between God and man. Our Intercessor! As children of God, we must first give Him our complete hearts and lives. We should accept Him as Savior and Lord. We should pray His promises in order to see them come to pass. We must be obedient to His instructions in His Word to build a personal relationship with Him. We must believe what He did on the cross for us. This belief will open the doors to promises. Speak out the scriptures when you pray. Your blessings are in the Word.

Let not your heart be troubledly believe in God, believe also in me. In my Father's house are many mansions: if it were not so, I would have told you. I go to prepare a place for you. And if I go and prepare a place for you, I will come again, and receive you unto myself; that where I am, there ye may be also. And whither I go ye know, and the way ye know. Thomas saith unto him, Lord, we know not whither thou goest; and how can we know the way?

John 14:1-5

Repeat this scripture in your prayers and be sure to let not your heart be troubled. Believe in God! Believe also in Jesus. Remember, the Father has a house and it is filled with many mansions and one of them He has prepared for you. If that was not so, He would have never told you. This is one of the reasons He is not hear today in flesh. He has gone on

The More I Pray

to prepare a place for you and me. One day He will fulfill His promise and come again and receive us to Him.

Honour thy father and mother; which is the first commandment with promise; That it may be well with thee, and thou mayest live long on the earth.

Ephesians 6:2,3

Many teens and young adults in the world die early because they never use this God given recipe for long life.

Another promise to be fulfilled just in honoring!

But seek ye first the kingdom of God and his righteousness and all other things shall be added unto you.

Matthew 6:33

These are just a few scriptures to use to pray the promises in Jesus' name. The promises the Father has for us both in this life and the life that has been prepared before the foundation of this world. He is not trying to put it together now as we go along the way and we somehow stumble over it. That's not how it works. We must ask for it in the right way even though its ours.

Ask, and it shall be given you; seek, and ye shall find; knock, and it shall be opened unto you:

Matthew 7:7

Ask in Jesus' name when we go through tests and trials. Jesus is the victorious One. He is the resurrected One! When we speak His name (we who have Him living on the inside) we receive His power and receive great results. He is

The More I Pray

Jesus Christ! The anointed One.   We receive the anointing from the Father through Jesus! That is why we come to the Father through Jesus, His only Son.

I and the Father are one. John 10:30

From this oneness is the power over everything and the power stands against, principalities, powers, rulers of darkness and Spiritual wickedness in high places. Prepare yourself to fight these battles. Suit up in your warfare clothes.

Finally, my brethren, be strong in the Lord, and in the power of his might. Put on the whole armour of God, that ye may be able to stand against the wiles of the devil. For we wrestle not against flesh and blood, but against principalities, against powers, against the rulers of the darkness of this world, against spiritual wickedness in high [places]. Wherefore take unto you the whole armour of God, that ye may be able to withstand in the evil day, and having done all, to stand. Stand therefore, having your loins girt about with truth, and having on the breastplate of righteousness; And your feet shod with the preparation of the gospel of peace; Above all, taking the shield of faith, wherewith ye shall be able to quench all the fiery darts of the wicked. And take the helmet of salvation, and the sword of the Spirit, which is the word of God: Praying always with all prayer and supplication in the Spirit and watching thereunto with all perseverance and supplication for all saints.

Ephesians 6:10-18

The More I Pray

There is no other name under heaven given among men whereby we must be saved but the name Jesus. Amen.

If the Son therefore shall make you free, ye shall be free indeed."

John 8:36

Chapter Six

Thy Kingdom Come, Thy Will Be Done on Earth As It Is In Heaven

And when he was demanded of the Pharisees, when the kingdom of God should come, he answered them and said, The kingdom of God cometh not with observation: Neither shall they say, Lo here! or, lo there! for, behold, the kingdom of God is within you.

Luke 17:20,21

This means God's sovereignty. His rule and reign, supremeness, supernatural power, dominion and authority, places Him in total command of everything. His divinity super-cedes our humanity. When we believe and accept Jesus into our hearts and life, He abides in us. He is the King of Kings operating in His Kingdom from within us who are saved and have become saints. The kingdom is not a building made with hands. It's not a visible picture with a size, shape, or color. It's not in the mountains or in the valley. There is no email address or a phone number to call. The Kingdom of God is not a place.

Giving thanks unto the Father, which hath made us meet to be partakers of the inheritance of the saints in light: Who hath delivered us from the power of darkness, and hath translated us into the kingdom of his dear Son: In whom we have redemption through his blood, even the forgiveness of sins: Who is the image of the invisible God,

The More I Pray

the firstborn of every creature: For by him were all things created, that are in heaven, and that are in earth, visible and invisible, whether they be thrones, or dominions, or principalities, or powers: all things were created by him, and for him: And he is before all things, and by him all things consist.

Colossians 1:12-17

When you invited Jesus into your heart, He brought His sovereignty with Him. Now you have Him living inside. His way, will, Word, authority, power, and dominion all now belongs to you.

In those days came John the Baptist, preaching in the wilderness of Judaea, and saying, Repent ye: for the kingdom of heaven is at hand. For this is he that was spoken of by the prophet Esaias, saying, the voice of one crying in the wilderness. Prepare ye the way of the Lord, make his paths straight.

Matthew 3:1-3

In those days John the Baptist preached and taught in the wilderness of Judea.

As soon as Jesus was baptized, he went up out of the water. At that moment heaven was opened, and he saw the Spirit of God descending like a dove and alighting on him. And a voice from heaven said, "This is my Son, whom I love; with him I am well pleased."

Matthew 3:16-17

With this kind of revelation, you can pray with understanding and receive answers to your prayers.

The More I Pray

But seek ye first the kingdom of God and his righteousness and all other things shall be added unto you.

Matthew 6:33

Now that you have learned some scriptures and have it in heart and mind continue to feed yourself by continuing to read the Word because, as a child of God, your body has become the temple of the living God. You need temple food for the Holy Spirit to be pleased and satisfied. When you pray *thy kingdom come*, we are asking God to change our way of thinking, our actions, behavior patterns, bad habits and attitudes. They all must go. John the Baptist message was *repent*. Jesus Himself said repent. His message is the same today like it was and will always be. Apostle Paul, whom God chose (Romans 12:1,2) says, "Our minds must be renewed with the Word of God so that your life will be transformed totally. When you study the scriptures to understand how to apply them to your prayer life daily, these are steps that will produce obedience to God's Word. This means to be changed from the inside out. It's a heart, mind and Spiritual change. It's to first change the way you think of God, the way you think of yourself, how you think of the Word and how you think of others.

For as he thinketh in his heart, so is he: Eat and drink, saith he to thee; but his heart is not with thee.

Proverbs 23:7

Study to shew thyself approved unto God, a workman that needeth not to be ashamed, rightly dividing the word of truth.

2 Timothy 2:15

.

The More I Pray

Your prayers will bring a presence which produces His Spirit which gives the power to us.

Then he answered and spake unto me, saying, this *is* the word of the LORD unto Zerubbabel, saying, Not by might, nor by power, but by my spirit, saith the LORD of hosts.

Zachariah 4:6

God's kingdom is a representation of His presence with you. His constant presence has a divine difference according to our prayers.

…thy will be done on earth as it is in heaven

Matthew 6:10

How would you know God's will for your life if you do not read and study the Bible? The Bible is God's manual to man. We who are chosen to have a responsibility to search and read scriptures and study, pray and ask in faith, believing trusting and discovering God's will for our lives. This special time and commitment should be a habit.

Then the word of the LORD came unto me, saying, Before I formed thee in the belly, I knew thee; and before thou camest forth out of the womb I sanctified thee, and I ordained thee a prophet unto the nations.

Jeremiah 1:4-5

For I know the plans I have for you," declares the LORD, "plans to prosper you and not to harm you, plans to give you hope and a future. **Then shall ye call upon me, and ye shall go and pray unto me, and I will hearken unto you**

Jeremiah 29:11,12

The More I Pray

It is important that we know and discover His divine will for us. He gives instructions in His Word. He said we must call upon Him then go and pray for the purposes, promises and for His will which is hidden in His Word.

In the beginning was the Word, and the Word was with God, and the Word was God. The same was in the beginning with God. All things were made by him; and without him was not anything made that was made. In him was life; and the life was the light of men.

John 1:1-4

We must escapade the scriptures by exploring, examining, investigating, observing, studying, and discovering all the things we need to effectively meditate in prayer. This will assist to make your prayers heard by God. Let your words be meaningful, not empty, powerless, and faithless. Words with no Spiritual value will never connect with the promises for your life.

But when ye pray, use not vain repetitions, as the heathen do: for they think that they shall be heard for their much speaking.

Matthew 6:7

Knowing God's will for your life is one of the most important things all should experience. We need to know what the Bible says. For instance, Romans 8: 27-28 reads, "And he that searcheth the hearts knoweth what is the mind of the Spirit, because he maketh intercession for the saints according to the will of God. And we know that all things work together for good to them that love God, to them who are the called according to his purpose."

Before the foundation of the earth, God had a plan and a purpose for those whom He has chosen. It's called

The More I Pray

God's Divine will. He is God of purpose, plan, design and destiny. To discover His will, we must be determined to use His Word daily. He wants to hear our hearts engage wholeheartedly in the scriptures that contain the promises He made to us so that He can answer our prayers. God's Word for His children are wrapped up in His Word. It's our responsibility to discover it as we read, study and consider it.

Prayer is also a sign of obedience. Spend time daily in the presence of God. If you needed to extract juice from an orange, you would first cut the orange in the correct way and use your strength to squeeze the orange. You may even go as far as to purchase an orange squeezer. Either way, the result is to get all the juice from it. Remember where you got the juice from. The orange! Jesus (The Word) is your juice source. Like the orange, the Word contains the promises of God for us in it.

Chapter Seven

Give Us This Day
Our Daily Bread

We must pray with an understanding, Jesus said:

"I am the bread of life." (John 6:33-35) "For the bread of God is He, who cometh down from Heaven and giveth life unto the world. Then the disciples said unto Him Lord, evermore give us this bread. And Jesus said I am the bread of life, he that cometh to me shall never hunger and he that believeth on me shall never thirst."

We know the bread in the natural is food that we eat to make us full and satisfy our hunger. We also know that the bread is flour that is made sometimes of wheat which is a heavy solid dough. It is made with water and baked. It is a general substance.

But he answered and said, it is written, Man shall not live by bread alone, but by every word that proceedeth out of the mouth of God.

Matthew 4:4

Jesus is referring to Himself as the Spiritual Bread who came down from Heaven to earth for a special reason. To give us new life and life more abundantly.

In him was life; and the life was the light of men.

John 1:4.

In Him was life for men. Jesus being the Spiritual bread is the nourishment that we need to digest daily. We must

The More I Pray

know that feasting on Spiritual food will change our character to one that reflects Jesus. That's only if we are living obediently.

"Thy word have I hid in my heart, that I might not sin against thee."

Psalm 119:11

When we eat Spiritual bread (the Word) It satisfies our body, mind, soul and Spirit. Our health, strength, wealth and wellbeing depend on it. It takes care of our mental, physical, Spiritual, and supernatural being. It's a daily nutrient that nourishes and flourishes the heart and the mind. A Spiritual meal keeps our conscience clear, clean, and without guilt and condemnation.

There is therefore now no condemnation to them which are in Christ Jesus, who walk not after the flesh, but after the Spirit.

Roman 8:1

The Word we feed on serves as a daily cleanser from wickedness that breathes sin into our lives. Jesus was always obedient to His Father. He always prayed to His Father. Jesus remained faithful, humble, loving, kind, compassionate, generous, merciful, forgiving, truthful and powerful. He did whatever His Father instructed Him to do. He was always peaceful and confident, trustworthy and most of all depending totally on His Father.

For the life He gave to us, which was a resurrected and new life. In 1 Corinthians 11:23, Jesus refers to Bread as His Body broken for us and the cup which represents His Blood shed for us. The word satisfies, heals, delivers, deliberates, creates, stimulates, elevates, educates, the truth of the Word. It sets us totally free from sin and iniquity. The Word washes and prospers us. When we eat food that is not good for our

The More I Pray

bodies, we become unhealthy. When we put drugs and alcohol in our bodies, use our bodies for sexual misconduct, cut ourselves and mark our bodies for and defile the temple of God we destroy ourselves.

Or do you not know that your body is the temple of the Holy Spirit *who is* in you, whom you have from God, and you are not your own? For you were bought at a price; therefore, glorify God in your body and in your spirit, which are God's.

1 Corinthians 6:19

These bad habits and practices cause us to sin. But when we eat the Word daily and obey the instructions and directions, we are feeding our Spirit, soul, and body with the right kinds of food. Instead of sinning we become righteous and Holy through the Holy Ghost. Give us this day, our daily Bread is for blessings to be released upon us daily. Your blessing! They surround us with your Holy Spirit, empower and enable us to do what we are called to do.

R - Righteousness- let goodness and mercy
     follow us daily.
E - Enjoy- let us enjoy daily what we do for
     God and others.
A - Anoint our head with oil, let us think right
     and keep our mind in perfect peace.
D - Desire the word daily

"My feet has held his steps, his way have I kept and not declined. Neither have I gone back from the commandment of his lips. I have esteemed the word of his mouth more than my necessary food."

Job 23:11-12

The More I Pray

Chapter Eight
And Forgive Us Our Debts As We Forgive Our Debtors

"For all have sinned and come short of the Glory of God."

Romans 3:23

"If we forgive men of their trespasses, your heavenly Father will also forgive you. But if you don't forgive men of their trespasses, neither will your Father forgive your trespasses."

Matthew 6:14-15

We must pray with understanding. Pray to the Father in Jesus and ask the Holy Spirit to help you to forgive those who hurt you. Also, ask Him to help those who you hurt to forgive you as well.   Pray and ask God to forgive us for our sins because, we sin consciously, unconsciously, and sometimes presumptuously, even with our tongues. We say things that are not kind to other people and about other people. When others say unkind things about us or to us, we must be ready to forgive them. This is what James said.

And the tongue is a fire, a world of iniquity so is the tongue among our members, that it defileth the whole body, and setteth on fire the course of nature; and it is set on fire of hell. For every kind of beasts, and of birds, and of serpents, and of things in the sea, is tamed, and hath been tamed of mankind: But the tongue can no man tame; it is an unruly evil, full of deadly poison. Therewith bless we God, even the Father; and therewith curse we men, which are made after the

The More I Pray

similitude of God. Out of the same mouth proceedeth blessing and cursing. My brethren, these things ought not so to be.

James 3:6-10

We cannot forgive by ourselves. We need the Holy Spirit to help us.

"Then came peter to Jesus and said, Lord how often shall my brother sin against me and I shall forgive Him? seven times? Jesus said unto Him, Not unto seven time but seventy time seven."

Matthew 18:21-22

Read the story in Matthew 18:21-35:

Then came Peter to him, and said, Lord, how oft shall my brother sin against me, and I forgive him? till seven times? Jesus saith unto him, I say not unto thee, Until seven times: but, Until seventy times seven. Therefore, is the kingdom of heaven likened unto a certain king, which would take account of his servants. And when he had begun to reckon, one was brought unto him, which owed him ten thousand talents. But forasmuch as he had not to pay, his lord commanded him to be sold, and his wife, and children, and all that he had, and payment to be made. The servant therefore fell down, and worshipped him, saying, Lord, have patience with me, and I will pay thee all. Then the lord of that servant was moved with compassion, and loosed him, and forgave him the debt. But the same servant went out, and found one of his fellow servants, which owed him a hundred pence: and he laid hands on him, and took him by the throat, saying, Pay me that thou owest. And his fellow servant fell down at his feet, and besought him, saying, have patience with

The More I Pray

me, and I will pay thee all. And he would not: but went and cast him into prison, till he should pay the debt. So, when his fellow servants saw what was done, they were very sorry, and came and told unto their lord all that was done. Then his lord, after that he had called him, said unto him, O thou wicked servant, I forgave thee all that debt, because thou desired me: Shouldest not thou also have had compassion on thy fellow servant, even as I had pity on thee? And his lord was wroth, and delivered him to the tormentors, till he should pay all that was due unto him. So likewise, shall my heavenly Father do also unto you, if ye from your hearts forgive not everyone his brother their trespasses.

Matthew 18:21-35

It is time to realize there are too many of us living with unforgiveness in our hearts and we are not aware of the damages that it has caused us and others. Most of the sicknesses and diseases in this world today are caused by unforgiveness. You would be shocked to know that Christians are at the top of the list. Most marriages, family breakups, disagreements, anger and fear in relationships are caused because of unforgiveness. It is a sin and it is spreading like wildfire. God's people must make a difference in the world. Doctors are finding more and more medicine to treat the symptoms of all illnesses because they are trained to treat what they can see, feel, hear, touch, and hold, but cannot discern what's in the heart of man. The Bible says,

"The heart is deceitful above all things, and desperately wicked: who can know it?" (Jeremiah 17:9)

The More I Pray

Chapter Nine

Lead us not into Temptation

Pray with understanding.

Then was Jesus led up of the Spirit into the wilderness to be tempted of the devil. And when he had fasted forty days and forty nights, he was afterward an hungred. And when the tempter came to him, he said, if thou be the Son of God, command that these stones be made bread. But he answered and said, it is written, Man shall not live by bread alone, but by every word that proceedeth out of the mouth of God. Then the devil taketh him up into the holy city, and setteth him on a pinnacle of the temple, And saith unto him, If thou be the Son of God, cast thyself down: for it is written, He shall give his angels charge concerning thee: and in their hands they shall bear thee up, lest at any time thou dash thy foot against a stone. Jesus said unto him, it is written again, Thou shalt not tempt the Lord thy God. Again, the devil taketh him up into an exceeding high mountain, and sheweth him all the kingdoms of the world, and the glory of them; And saith unto him, all these things will I give thee, if thou wilt fall down and worship me. Then saith Jesus unto him, get thee hence, Satan: for it is written, thou shalt worship the Lord thy God, and him only shalt thou serve. Then the devil leaveth him, and, behold, angels came and ministered unto him.

Matthew 4:1-11

As Christians we are followers of Christ. We must read the Bible daily, study the scriptures, meditate, and hide the Word in the secret place.

The More I Pray

Thy word have I hid in mine heart, that I might not sin against thee.

Psalm 119:11

"Let the word of Christ dwell in you daily, teaching and admonishing one another in psalms and hymns and Spiritual songs. Singing with grace in your hearts to the lord."

Colossians 3:16

Therefore, we must know what the scripture teaches. Jesus was and still is the Son of God and He was tempted by the devil. We too will be tempted by the devil. As a child of God, we would have to do exactly what Jesus did when He was tempted by the devil. He did not yield to the temptations of the devil. Instead He lived within His identity. He knew the scriptures. He knew His purpose for coming to earth and He knew who His Father was. He knew who Satan was too. He knew Satan was real. Jesus had finished forty days of fasting and was hungry. Satan knew it and took the opportunity to tempt Jesus. But Jesus had the Holy Spirit's power to resist. Jesus is the Lord's anointed One. After forty days of fasting, Jesus was prepared in His Spirit and fully loaded with the power of God from His Father. He could not yield to temptation because He was in the perfect will of God. He was at the right place, at the right time, and doing the right thing. Jesus spoke the Word with authority to the devil every time He was tempted by him. This is what you and I need to understand. We too can resist temptation of the devil, just like Jesus did. The same power that His Father gave, Jesus took it and gave it unto His followers and us.

But ye shall receive power, after that the Holy Ghost is come upon you: and ye shall be witnesses unto me both in Jerusalem, and in all Judaea, and in Samaria, and unto the uttermost part of the earth.

The More I Pray

Acts 1:8

Listen to what James 1:12-15 says, "Blessed is the man that endureth temptation, for when he is tried, he shall receive the crown of life. Which the lord has promised to them who love Him. Let no man say when he is tempted, I am tempted of God, for God cannot be tempted with evil, neither tempt he any man. But every man is tempted when he is drawn away by his own lust and entice. When lust is conceived it bringeth forth sin and sin, when it is finished bringeth forth death." *But deliver us from evil.* As Christians we always think that the Bible is referring to sinners alone when talking about sin. You don't have to warn sinners about sin. That's what they do. But we that are righteous must pray to be delivered from evil because Jeremiah 17:9 says, "The heart is deceitful above all things, and desperately wicked: who can know it?" We must guard our hearts from evil because out of the abundance of the heart the mouth speaks according to Matthew 12:34.

"Evil communication corrupts good manners."
1 Corinthians 15:33

"Beloveth follow not that which is evil but that which is good. He that doeth good is of God but he that doeth evil hath not seen God."
3 John 1:11

"Who so rewardeth evil for good, evil shall not depart from his house."
Proverb 17:13

This is what the old testament prophet says:

The More I Pray

"Hate the evil and love the good, and establish judgement at the gate, it might be that the Lord God of host will be gracious unto the remnant of Joseph."

Amos 5:15

"Seek good and not evil, that you may live, and that the God of host shall be with you as he has spoken."

Amos 5:14

There are scriptures for every situation, condition, problem and circumstance that we will face on our journeys. God has already prepared divine destinies for all of us. The more scriptures we learn, the more we earn the right to practice them in our daily prayer. Our unique ways lay the foundation for answered prayers. When we begin to hate evil, there is a transformation that takes place in our minds and Spirit. When we allow the Holy Spirit to take complete control over our will and emotions, we can then surrender our thoughts and bring down every evil imagination.

Paul's writings to the church of Thessalonica says:

See that none render evil for evil unto any man; but ever follow that which is good, both among yourselves, and to all men. Rejoice evermore. Pray without ceasing. In everything give thanks: for this is the will of God in Christ Jesus concerning you. Quench not the Spirit. Despise not prophesyings. Prove all things; hold fast that which is good. Abstain from all appearance of evil. 1

Thessalonians 5:15-22

Chapter Ten

For thine is the Kingdom, The Power and The Glory Forever! Amen

"For thine is the kingdom, The Power and The Glory forever. Amen."

Matthew 6:13

When we get down to praying, know that the kingdom of God is ruled by God Himself. He is the king of His Kingdom. All power, glory, and all honor belong to Him. He is the King of Kings and Lord of Lords. He is Alpha and Omega. He is the beginning and the end. He is God almighty. He rules in the heavens and He rules in the earth. He reigns and rules now and forever. When you get down to pray, you're not praying to an idol, nor a statue of liberty, nor are you praying to a man. God is not a figment of your imagination. God is real! He is not a thing. He is a Spirit (John 4:4). His very presence is alive in us and for us who are born again. His Spirit lives in us.

"And when he Jesus was demanded of the Pharisees, when the kingdom of God should come? Jesus answered them and said, The kingdom of God cometh not with visible signs and observation. Neither shall they say here or there is the kingdom."

Luke 17:20

We, who are chosen of the Lord, have the kingdom of God in us. God has prepared a place for the Holy Spirit to live. That place is in our hearts.

"There was a man of the pharisees named Nicodemus, a ruler of the Jews, came to Jesus by night and said unto

The More I Pray

Him, Jesus, we know that thine are a teacher come from God for no man can do these miracles that thine doeth except God be with them. Jesus answered and said, except a man be born again he cannot see the kingdom of God."

John 3:1-3

"Unless a man be born of water and of the Spirit he cannot answer into the kingdom of God."

John 3:5

Before we can see things, the way God sees them, we must be reborn from within. That is why Jesus said we must be born again. Though our natural birth came first, there is nothing Spiritual in us that will empower or enable us to become disciples. Natural man cannot be transformed by natural means. (Matthew 4:4). To be born again means to be born a second time, not in the flesh, but in the Spirit. To be baptized in water and in the Holy Spirit, and with fire means to be filled through the baptism of the Holy Spirit. There is an anointing that is of the Holy Spirit that causes the supernatural to happen. Don't you know that Jesus is the anointed one and we cannot stay in our natural state of mind to serve Him. "Behold I stand at the door and knock, if any man hears my voice I will come in and sup with Him and Him with me (Revelation 3:20). Jesus comes into our hearts by way of invitation. When He comes, He expects us to repent of your sins. The Holy Spirit is the one who reveals the truth. We must allow Him to work on our hearts.

"I am the way, the truth and the light, no man cometh unto the Father but by me."

John 14:16

Seek he first the kingdom of God and his righteousness.

Matthew 6:33

The More I Pray

The Word of God must be spoken in all our prayers for daily living. Those who will enter the Kingdom of God must allow God to rule and reign in all life's affairs. Obedience is the key word. Jesus warned his disciples not to pray like the hypocrites who prayed to be seen and to be heard but, was never obedient to the scriptures. They were just religious. Jesus taught his disciples to pray righteously. Pray the scriptures, Matthew 6:7. The Father wants us to pray like Jesus taught his disciples to pray. We his disciples must obey all his instructions and directions and not just listen and hear. Do what they say. The Words in the Bible are not man's word but are God's. Are you one of God's people? We all should have a desire to exercise His rules. Jesus should be our top priority for all our life. His love for us is unconditional. Therefore, He takes His responsibility concerning us lovingly and seriously. He wants us also to take up our responsibility in the decision we have made and base them on the relationship between us and His promises. He has great blessings in store for His children. All His promises are yes and AMEN!

www.ingramcontent.com/pod-product-compliance
Lightning Source LLC
Chambersburg PA
CBHW061054050726
47592CB00004B/1672